History of America

The Spanish
in Early America

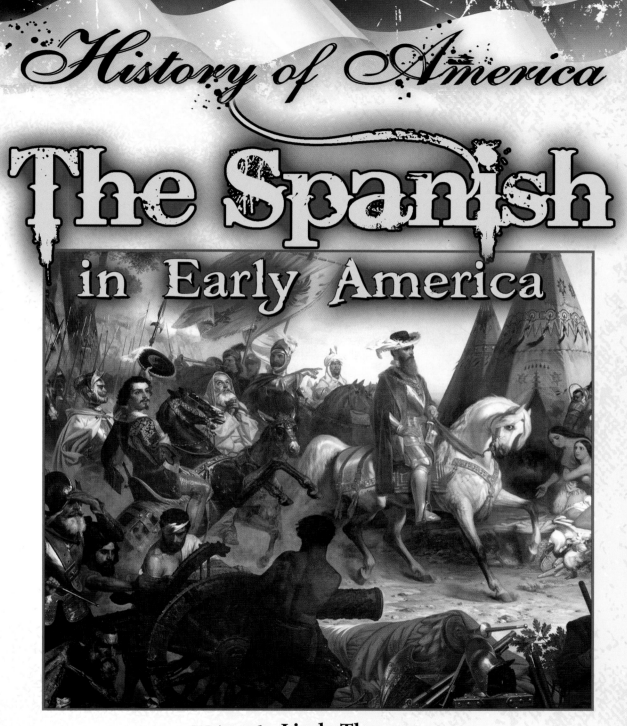

Written by **Linda Thompson**

rourkeeducationalmedia.com

www.rourkeeducationalmedia.com

PHOTO CREDITS: Bonsal, Stephen, Edward Fitzgerald Beale, 1912: page 32; Courtesy Library of Congress, Edward S. Curtis Collection: pages 13, 18; Courtesy Library of Congress, Prints and Photographs Division: Title Page, pages 5, 6, 7, 9, 14, 15, 20, 21, 27, 28, 34, 37, 39, 40, 41; Courtesy Library of Congress, Rare Books and Special Collections Division: pages 25, 33; Courtesy NASA: page 31; Courtesy National Oceanic and Atmospheric Administration: pages 4, 35, 43; Courtesy National Parks Service: page 12; Courtesy Rohm Padilla: pages 26, 32, 42; Courtesy Charles Reasoner: pages 10, 22, 23; Courtesy U.S. Army, Center of Military History: pages 19, 29; Courtesy U.S. Department of the Interior, U.S. Geological Survey: page 30.

Edited by Jill Sherman

Cover design by Nicola Stratford, bdpublishing.com

Interior layout by Tara Raymo

Library of Congress PCN Data

Thompson, Linda
The Spanish in Early America / Linda Thompson.
ISBN 978-1-62169-841-8 (hard cover)
ISBN 978-1-62169-736-7 (soft cover)
ISBN 978-1-62169-945-3 (e-Book)
Library of Congress Control Number: 2013936392

Also Available as:

ROURKE'S
e-Books

Rourke Educational Media
Printed in the United States of America,
North Mankato, Minnesota

Rourke

Table of Contents

Chapter 1
Discovery of Florida

The first European attempt at a settlement in what became the United States was made in 1526, only 34 years after Christopher Columbus first landed in the New World. This settlement was San Miguel de Guadalupe, founded by Spain on North America's Atlantic coast. It happened nearly 60 years before the founding of Roanoke, which is often considered the first settlement in North America.

The Old City Gates, once the only entrance into St. Augustine, are now a landmark of the St. Augustine Historic District.

Like Roanoke, San Miguel de Gualdape was doomed to fail. The dream of a Spanish lawyer named Lucas Vásquez de Ayllón, the outpost lasted only two months. Native American attacks, disease, their leader's death, and conflict with each other proved too much for these settlers as they struggled to exist on the coast of what is now Georgia or southern South Carolina. Of the 500 people who sailed from the settlement of Santo Domingo in the West Indies, only 150 survived to return.

After that failure, Spain made several more attempts at establishing a foothold on the Florida coast and finally succeeded. St. Augustine, Florida, about 40 miles (64 kilometers) south of today's Jacksonville, is the oldest permanent European settlement in the United States. It was founded as San Augustín on September 8, 1565. The founder, Pedro Menéndez de Avilés, claimed this sheltered harbor and all of the land called "La Florida" in the name of his king, Felipe II.

Pedro Menéndez de Avilés (1519-1574)

Juan Ponce de León (1474-1521)

THE NAME OF "LA FLORIDA"

Juan Ponce de León first saw Florida shores on April 2, 1513. Easter was coming so he named the land Pascua Florida, or Floral Easter. It became known as La Florida. No written records exist to confirm the popular legend that Ponce was searching for a fountain of youth.

All of Spain's explorations and early colonizing were linked to spreading the Roman Catholic faith. The Spanish king and **conquistadors** saw themselves as agents of the Catholic Church in America, viewing other **sects** as a threat to the true religion. They believed that having left the Catholic Church, Protestants were guilty of rebellion and could expect no mercy, as Felipe II had written.

A carving showing a Spanish priest and Native Americans planting a cross.

These beliefs help explain the cruel behavior of many of the early explorers, including Christopher Columbus. Many Europeans believed that Native Americans held the wrong ideas about religion, which needed to be changed. On Hispaniola, the

When Columbus and his sailors came ashore, the Arawaks ran to greet them carrying food, water, and gifts.

West Indies island Columbus first **colonized**, slavery, harsh punishment, and European diseases wiped out 200,000 of the 250,000 Arawak within 20 years.

Other explorers and settlers followed the example set by Columbus. These included Hernán Cortés in Mexico, Francisco Pizarro in Peru, English settlers in Virginia and Massachusetts, and Dutch colonists in New York. The Spaniards were mainly searching for God, gold, and glory. That meant converting Native Americans to Catholicism, finding gold and silver to take back to their king, and winning fame and honor for themselves. But another very important goal was finding land for people to live on.

Between 1519 and 1521 Hernán Cortés was defeating the Aztec empire in what is now Mexico. He founded a colony there, Nueva España, meaning New Spain, which lasted 300 years. By 1531 Francisco Pizarro had begun to conquer the Inca empire in present-day Peru. Within a few years, Mexico and Peru, with their rich deposits of gold and silver, were major sources of Spanish wealth and power in the New World.

As time passed, it was necessary to build more **fortresses** and towns in La Florida. From the 1550s on, French pirates raided Spanish ships loaded with gold and silver. Soon English pirates, such as Sir Francis Drake, were doing the same. The waters off Florida and the West Indies were favorite **marauding** spots.

Aztec pyramids date back to the 1400s. They originally served as religious centers and today stand in archaeological parks throughout Mexico.

Within a few years, Spain had built missions and small forts to protect them around the tip of Florida to the Gulf Coast. In 1573, a royal proclamation from the king gave missionaries an important role in exploring and settling new lands. Franciscan priests arrived to staff the missions and baptized thousands of Native Americans.

Francisco Pizarro (1471-1541)

In the early 1600s, Spain was considering abandoning La Florida, but the missionaries argued that the converts needed their spiritual leadership. They appealed to Felipe III and convinced him not to leave.

SPANISH LAST NAMES

Spanish last names usually consist of the father's last name followed by the mother's last name. As a shortened form, only the father's last name is used. Therefore, Pedro Menéndez de Avilés is known as Menéndez. There are exceptions to this rule. For example, Francisco Vásquez de Coronado is known as Coronado, his mother's name.

The adventure of Álvar Nuñez Cabeza de Vaca shows the difficulties Spain faced in its early colonizing attempts. Cabeza de Vaca accompanied Pánfilo de Narváez, who had permission from the king to settle lands along the coast of the Gulf of Mexico. In 1528 they landed south of Tampa Bay with about 390 men.

During eight years of traveling, Spanish explorer Álvar Nuñez Cabeza de Vaca became a slave, trader, and shaman to various Native American tribes.

By April 1529 only 14 men remained. None would have survived except that Cabeza de Vaca had learned the art of herbal healing, becoming known among the Native Americans as a medicine man. The small party traveled westward with a growing escort of Native Americans. They probably passed through land that is now southern New Mexico and Arizona.

In the spring of 1536, Cabeza de Vaca and three survivors walked into a village on Mexico's Pacific coast. There, Spaniards hunting for slaves to work in Mexico's silver mines were astounded to see four nearly naked men, one black and the others a deep bronze, arrive with a large group of Native American followers. The four continued on to Mexico City. They had come more than 3,500 miles (5,633 kilometers) in eight years!

Cabeza de Vaca wrote reports of his astonishing adventure. He described people living in villages in the land he had walked through, some with houses four or five stories high. These people practiced farming and traded in emeralds, turquoise stones, and buffalo robes. His stories attracted the attention of two powerful men in Mexico City, the **viceroy**, or governor, Antonio de Mendoza and Hernán Cortés. They would soon launch new expeditions to explore and settle the interior of North America.

Chapter 2
New Mexico

Besides Florida, Spain's major foothold in North America for 200 years was New Mexico. Like Florida, New Mexico was much larger than the present state of that name, reaching into areas that are now Arizona, Nevada, Utah, Colorado, and other states. Well into the 17th century, explorers of New Mexico discovered rumors of golden cities hidden nearby. Searching for these cities kept the Spaniards moving on rather than settling down.

Coronado National Memorial, Arizona.

Inspired by Cabeza de Vaca's reports, Antonio de Mendoza wanted to expand his **domain** north of Mexico. He could not convince Cabeza de Vaca or the other two Spaniards to return as guides, so he purchased a slave, Esteban, to take part in an expedition headed by Francisco Vásquez de Coronado in 1540.

In preparation for Coronado's journey, Mendoza sent Esteban with a party led by a Franciscan **friar**, Marcos de Niza. Within a year, Father Marcos returned with stories of rich kingdoms with jewel-covered temples and exotic animals such as camels and elephants. He called this land the Seven Cities of Cíbola. His stories encouraged Mendoza to speed up plans for the Coronado expedition.

Father Marcos had greatly exaggerated the terraced houses of the Zuni village. We now know that camels and elephants never lived in South America.

THE FATE OF ESTEBAN

Father Marcos had Esteban, the black slave, scout ahead with several hundred Native Americans. Esteban would send someone back with a white cross whenever he found something important. After Esteban sent back a very large cross, he was not heard from again. Later, it was learned that the Zuni had killed him. Their mud villages were probably the Seven Cities of Cíbola that Father Marcos described, though its unlikely Marcos had seen them himself.

Landing of de Soto in Florida.

Elsewhere, another conquistador had sailed from the West Indies to explore land west of Florida. Hernando Méndez de Soto had permission to explore and settle all of Florida. He and other Spaniards believed that La Florida stretched west to Mexico and north perhaps as far as Canada. With 600 men, de Soto marched across what is now the southeastern United States. In 1542, he became ill and died. Four months later, when his troops returned to Mexico, only half of them were still alive.

THE DEVASTATION CAUSED BY DE SOTO

De Soto passed through a region with large populations of Native Americans. His men were the only outsiders to see large populations of Apalachee, Cofitachequi, Coosa, Tascaloosa, and similar tribes living in prosperity before European diseases destroyed them. Many Native Americans fought the intruders, who took slaves, food, and supplies by force. Thousands of Native Americans died after the Spaniards had passed through because they had no **immunity** to diseases such as typhus, typhoid, smallpox, and measles.

Back in Mexico, Coronado began his trek in 1540, passing through what is now southern Arizona. When he reached the Zuni villages, he was disappointed to see two-story mud buildings rather than the fabled Cíbola. Coronado read the requerimiento to the Zuni. It was a strange ceremony Spanish conquerors had to perform in America, which told the inhabitants that God and the **Pope** had given the Americas to the king of Spain. Native Americans were ordered to submit to this authority and to agree to **convert** to Catholicism. If they refused, the Spaniards said, "we shall forcefully enter your country and make war against you in all ways."

The Coronado expedition enters New Mexico in 1540.

THE RIO GRANDE PUEBLOS

Early Spanish explorers came upon more than 100 settlements along the Rio Grande and called them "pueblos," meaning "villages." They were solidly built mud buildings, often two or three stories high, with central plazas. The people grew corn, squash, beans, and cotton. They hunted game and gathered wild plants to eat. They spoke at least nine different languages and had trade networks over long distances.

It is unlikely that the Zuni and other Native American groups understood this statement read to them in a foreign language. The Zuni resisted, firing arrows at the intruders. But Coronado took the village by force and made it his headquarters. Some of his men scouted the Rio Grande valley, visiting more than 100 pueblos between present-day Taos and Albuquerque, New Mexico, and eastward to Pecos, one of the largest pueblos.

Taos Pueblo is the only Native American community designated both a World Heritage Site and a National Historic Landmark. The adobe building has been inhabited for over 1,000 years.

Meanwhile, Viceroy Mendoza had become interested in the Pacific coast. He commissioned another Spaniard, Juan Rodríguez Cabrillo, to seek a water passage that might link the Atlantic and Pacific oceans. Cabrillo left Mexico's western coast in 1542, sailing north. Cabrillo and his men explored 1,200 miles (1,930 kilometers) of the Baja California and Alta California coastline, giving Spain a claim to the entire Pacific coast of North America. But Spain did not begin to colonize California for another 225 years.

New Mexico's first permanent European settlement came about in 1598. Juan Oñate y Salazar had been named governor and captain-general of all of New Mexico. He set out with about 500 people, determined to form a colony. About 25 miles (40 kilometers) from present El Paso, Texas, Oñate formally claimed the land for King Felipe II and himself.

THE OTHER FIRST THANKSGIVING

Near El Paso, Oñate's group rested for a week. The local Native Americans, whom they called Mansos, brought great quantities of fish in exchange for clothing and gifts. The feast that followed, 23 years before the more famous event at Plymouth Rock, is celebrated in El Paso as the first Thanksgiving in the United States.

In July 1598 Oñate established his first capital at a pueblo named Okhe, which he called San Juan de los Caballeros. Today this is San Juan Pueblo, north of Santa Fe. After a couple of months he moved across the river to Yungé pueblo, which Oñate named San Gabriel. From these bases, Franciscan friars spread out along the Rio Grande and began the process of conversion. At each pueblo Oñate read the requerimiento, later reporting to the king that all pueblo leaders had agreed to become subjects of Spain.

One and two story adobe homes were typical of southwest pueblos like San Juan Pueblo.

Oñate was often away on explorations and neglected San Gabriel. Lacking leadership, many of his colonists returned to Mexico. For this reason, and also his mistreatment of Native Ameicans, the king ordered that Oñate be replaced. The king considered abandoning New Mexico because, like Florida, it was a drain on the treasury. But in 1608, the Franciscan friars convinced the king to allow them to continue their **ministry** to the Native Americans. By 1629 Spain had more than 25 missions in New Mexico, with 50 priests and more than 60,000 baptized Native Americans practicing Christianity.

THE FOUNDING OF SANTA FE

Some of Oñate's settlers moved south from San Gabriel to what is now Santa Fe, New Mexico. In 1610, Oñate's successor, Pedro de Peralta, named it the Villa Real de Santa Fe. Santa Fe is the oldest capital city in the United States.

In the 1800s Santa Fe became a large trading area for supplies needed while traveling.

During the 1600s fewer than 2,000 Spaniards lived in Florida and probably fewer than 3,000 in New Mexico. But though they were few, Spaniards began to influence the large Native American populations in many ways. Native Americans did not give up their religions, but combined their beliefs with those taught by the missionaries. Native Americans also learned about cattle, horses, mules, sheep, goats, pigs, the plow, and wheat, which, unlike corn, could be grown in the winter. They learned to read and write Spanish, became blacksmiths and carpenters, and adopted new ways of weaving and cooking. The Spanish also learned from the Native Americans, and the blending of the two cultures created a unique way of life that endures today, especially in the Southwest.

Feast day at San Estevan del Rey Mission, Acoma Pueblo, New Mexico, where the mesa is opened to the public for a celebration.

Chapter 3

Native Americans Revolt

In both Florida and New Mexico, Spanish rule began to collapse in the late 17th century. One reason was that both church and government forced Native Americans to work hard without pay. Spaniards depended on Native American labor for their well-being. They had to build missions, farm fields, produce blankets and cloth, and otherwise contribute to the settlement's earnings. They were also forced to travel to areas where **nomadic** tribes held trade fairs. They had to **barter** for bison hides and deerskins and bring them back.

Inside a Native American blacksmith shop, Zuni Pueblo.

Timucuan men were forced to search for gold and natural resources in Florida.

In Florida, Native Americans struggled to build and supply more than 30 missions, growing food, cotton, and tobacco for the friars. They were forced to work on public projects. They repaired roads, built bridges, operated ferry services, unloaded ships, and accompanied wagon trains. They were paid little or nothing for these services. Some soldiers and settlers illegally forced Native Americans to work for them personally. An especially humiliating job was to serve as a human pack animal, hauling cargo.

Native Americans also suffered from **drought** and disease. In 1640, smallpox killed 3,000 Native Americans in New Mexico, nearly 10 percent of the entire pueblo population. Additional epidemics occurred in the 1660s. From 1667 to 1672, a lack of rain caused widespread starvation, with no crops harvested between 1665 and 1668. All of these forces led to an amazing event in 1680 called the Pueblo Revolt.

About 30,000 Pueblo lived in New Mexico, greatly outnumbering the 2,300 Spaniards. A San Juan Native American named Popé led a rebellion involving some 17,000 Indians. Planning the revolt and keeping it secret was a remarkable accomplishment because the Pueblo people spoke different languages and lived in more than two dozen villages spread over several hundred miles. Popé managed to unite most of the other Pueblos against the Spaniards. Some neighboring Apaches, who resented the colonists' practice of enslaving their people, also joined.

Pueblo revolt leader Popé (1630-1688).

The first church at Taos Pueblo was destroyed in the Pueblo Revolt. After being rebuilt in 1706, it was ruined again in 1847 by the U.S. military.

On August 9, 1680, Native Americans in Taos and San Juan began burning and looting churches and homes. Spanish arms and livestock were seized. Popé ordered every Catholic object destroyed because Native Americans were to return to their old religions. Baptisms were to be reversed. The revolt spread to the south, as well as to Zuni on the west and the Hopi villages in the north. Within a few days all of the missions had been destroyed, with 21 missionaries and nearly 400 **colonists** killed.

In 1680 Spain also began to lose power in La Florida. Eager to control the fur trade and the coastline, English settlers in Carolina allied with Native American tribes to drive out the Spaniards. By the end of 1706, they had wiped out all Florida missions except those near San Augustín. As in New Mexico, large numbers of Native Americans joined in the attacks and renounced Christianity. Unlike in New Mexico, however, Spain would not be able to reconquer its Florida colony.

The flight of Spanish colonists to El Paso prompted the first mission building in what is now Texas. More than 300 Native Americans who had fled with the Spaniards needed homes. In 1682 Franciscans founded several missions there, as well as in east Texas. They were most successful in the area of what is now San Antonio. The San Antonio de Valero mission, begun in 1718, would later become famous as "the Alamo." A **presidio**, or fort, was added to protect the mission. To populate San Antonio, Spain brought immigrants from its Canary Island colony, off the coast of northern Africa.

All the work in the missions were performed by the Native Americans who eagerly embraced their place in the Spanish empire.

By this time, the Spanish had retaken New Mexico. Spain sent a new commander to El Paso, Don Diego de Vargas. In 1692 Vargas took a small force, made up of a several missionaries and fewer than 200 soldiers, up the Rio Grande with a daring strategy. When he reached a pueblo, instead of attacking with guns he had his soldiers sing hymns and pray. With a fanfare of trumpets and drums, he **pacified** Native Americans of 23 pueblos and raised the Spanish flag. Returning to El Paso in December, he began to prepare for the reconquest.

Don Diego de Vargas (1643-1704)

In the fall of 1693, Vargas triumphantly led about 800 people back to New Mexico, but many Native Americans had changed their minds. The Spaniards spent a year fighting up and down the Rio Grande. As missions were rebuilt, Native Americans resisted, killing five more Franciscans in 1696. Gradually, however, the pueblos were brought under control except for the Hopi, who never did submit to the reconquest.

Chapter 4
Losing America

The 18th century saw Spain expanding into new regions of America as well as giving up land to its rivals. During this century, Spain's most important colonization efforts took place in California.

Spain sided with France in the French and Indian War, known as the Seven Years' War in Europe. France lost the war and signed the Treaty of Paris of 1763, which forced Spain to give La Florida to England. The English changed San Augustín's name to St. Augustine.

Defeat of General Braddock in the French and Indian War in 1755.

THE BACK AND FORTH OF FLORIDA

After Spain established Pensacola in 1698, it became the center of life in western Florida. When England acquired La Florida in 1763, the country divided it into two provinces, East Florida and West Florida. After the American Revolution, both Floridas were given back to Spain. Then, in 1819 the United States bought all of Florida for $5 million and made it a territory in 1821.

But Spain had won another prize, the vast region of Louisiana! France had transferred ownership through a secret treaty in 1762 to avoid losing it to England. Spain thought Louisiana would serve as a **buffer**, helping protect its western colonies, especially Nueva España.

The siege of Pensacola. Spanish troops in the foreground force the surrender of the British garrison.

Like the English, however, the French had sold arms to Native Americans, something that Spain had forbidden its settlers and traders to do. In Texas, Comanches and their allies, armed by the French, forced the abandonment of missions and presidios. Around San Antonio, the missions succeeded but they never drew more than a few hundred converts. Without Native American labor, the settlers did their own farming

José de Gálvez (1720-1787)

and ranching. These settlers were also few, with only about 1,200 living in the area in 1760.

With both France and England gaining ground, Spain increased its defenses across the frontier. In 1769, King Carlos III turned his attention to California. He sent José de Gálvez to make recommendations. Gálvez was especially interested in the northern frontier, where English and Russian fur traders operated. He suggested building missions and presidios from San Diego to Monterey Bay.

A 26-foot (8-meter) statue commemorates Junipero Serra, instrumental in the founding of the chain of Spanish mission churches along the California coast.

The Franciscan friar responsible for beginning to build Spanish missions in New California was Junípero Serra. This 55-year-old friar became one of the best known priests in American history. In 1769, he built the first of 21 missions, San Diego de Álcala. Meanwhile, Captain Gaspar de Portolá took 60 men by foot from San Diego to seek a trail for the friars to follow. He missed Monterey Bay and instead discovered San Francisco Bay. A year later, he reached Monterey and built a presidio with a mission attached. In 1777 Monterey was named the capital of New California.

The biggest challenge in California was getting food and supplies to the settlements. Some ships were wrecked in storms while men waiting on the coast died of scurvy and hunger. Gálvez understood that if the missions were to flourish, he would have to find a dependable overland route and bring families, single women, livestock, and supplies from Sonora, a Mexican province south of Arizona.

In January 1774, Captain Juan Bautista de Anza left Sonora with 34 men to search for an overland route to the California coast. They crossed the Colorado River and continued to Monterey. In 1775, Anza led a group of 240 men and women over this route. Some settled in Monterey, while others moved north to become the first San Francisco colonists.

SAN FRANCISCO BAY

MONTEREY BAY

The northern California coast is characterized by rocky beaches and cliff sides. The inhospitable land prevented large European settlements for many years.

In the early 1800s, San Francisco was populated with missions and homesteads until the Gold Rush in 1849.

In 1781, however, the Yuma tribe closed the Colorado River crossing and it stayed closed for 40 years. Fortunately, mission farming had become successful within the few years that the land route had been open. After 1781, Spanish settlements in California depended on food that the missions produced or brought from Mexico once or twice a year by ship.

By the time Serra died in 1784, nine missions had been built in a 550 mile (885 kilometer) long chain. Under his **successors**, 11 more were built. More than 21,000 Native Americans lived at the missions. The last mission, San Francisco Solano, in the town of Sonoma, was not built until 1823, after Mexico had won its independence from Spain.

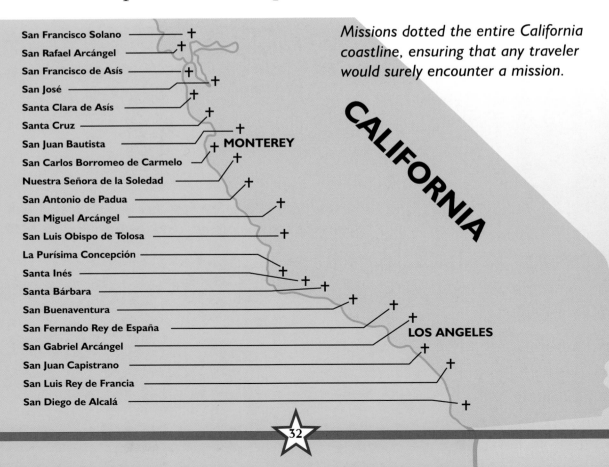

San Francisco Solano
San Rafael Arcángel
San Francisco de Asís
San José
Santa Clara de Asís
Santa Cruz
San Juan Bautista
San Carlos Borromeo de Carmelo
Nuestra Señora de la Soledad
San Antonio de Padua
San Miguel Arcángel
San Luis Obispo de Tolosa
La Purísima Concepción
Santa Inés
Santa Bárbara
San Buenaventura
San Fernando Rey de España
San Gabriel Arcángel
San Juan Capistrano
San Luis Rey de Francia
San Diego de Alcalá

MONTEREY

CALIFORNIA

LOS ANGELES

Missions dotted the entire California coastline, ensuring that any traveler would surely encounter a mission.

THE CALIFORNIOS

By 1800, there were about 1,800 Hispanic people in Alta California. These included Spaniards, **criollos**, and **mestizos**. All of them lived along the 500 mile (805 kilometer) coastal region between San Diego and San Francisco. Most lived in California's three towns, Los Angeles, San Jose, and Branciforte, which became Santa Cruz. However, some smaller populations lived near the four military presidios: San Diego, Santa Barbara, Monterey, and San Francisco.

Hauling water and washing clothes was an important role of women in California during the 1800s.

President Thomas Jefferson (1743-1826)

A major event in 1783 set the stage for the closing years of Spain's North American empire. The United States of America was born! Through its alliance with France, Spain had sided with the colonies in the American Revolution. On September 3, 1783, the United States formally returned both Florida provinces to Spain. For a few years afterward, Spain's colonies formed an unbroken band from the Atlantic to the Pacific along the southern U.S. border. But within 38 years, these possessions would all be lost.

It began with the purchase of Louisiana by Thomas Jefferson in 1803. The Spanish king had returned the vast territory to France in 1800 in a secret swap for land in Italy that never came to pass. So when the emperor of France, Napoleon Bonaparte, decided to sell Louisiana to Jefferson, there was nothing Spain could do.

The forts in Florida, meanwhile, had fallen into decay under British control. American frontiersmen had pushed across the borders and set up homesteads in West Florida. They began appealing to the United States for **annexation**, and in 1810 the United States took West Florida over the protests of Spain. On February 2, 1819, Spain signed a treaty that transferred all of La Florida to the United States.

For years, Spanish Americans had been developing an identity separate from Spaniards. In 1808, Napoleon Bonaparte seized Spain. He was removed in 1814, but during his short rule, Spain's South American colonies began declaring their independence. On September 16, 1810, a friar named Miguel Hidalgo y Costilla and several hundred of his parishioners seized a prison at Dolores, Mexico, beginning Mexico's struggle for independence.

The Fort in St. Augustine Florida, a monument of human determination and endurance, is visited today. Guests experience its history through live demonstrations and interactive activities.

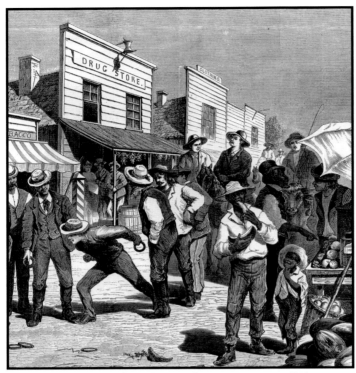

In the 1800s, before Texas became part of the United States, it was populated with Spanish-born Tejenos and American settlers.

The Treaty of Córdoba of 1821 gave Mexico its independence. In North America, provinces that had belonged to Spain, such as Alta, California, New Mexico, and Texas were now part of Mexico. The region was still very remote from its capital, which was now Mexico City. Thinly populated and weakly defended, it was ripe for takeover by the United States.

To help populate the empty plains, Spain had encouraged Americans to move into Texas. In 1820, Moses Austin had won permission to establish a colony of non-Hispanic Americans there. This changed Spain's earlier policies, under which foreigners were unwelcome in Spain's territories. By 1836 Texas had about 35,000 non-Hispanic colonists, outnumbering Hispanic people by about 10 to 1.

THE ALAMO

In 1835 border **skirmishes** began between Texans and Mexicans trying to defend their missions around San Antonio. Antonio López de Santa Anna, a Mexican general, fought against the Texans. At Mission San Antonio, now renamed the Alamo, he found 187 men defending it. In an extremely bloody battle, all 187 were killed, including Davy Crockett. But the Texans retaliated at the Battle of San Jacinto, capturing Santa Anna and forcing him to surrender. On May 14, 1836, the Republic of Texas was born.

Antonio López de Santa Anna (1794-1876)

The Alamo was originally called San Antonio de Valero. It was later called Alamo, the Spanish name for the cottonwood trees surrounding the mission.

Texas declared independence from Mexico in 1837 and then spent eight years as the Lone Star Republic. The Texans petitioned the United States for annexation, but anti-slavery Congressmen rejected early requests to annex Texas.

When Mexico became independent, foreigners were no longer discouraged. Mexico desired foreign trade, and soon wagon trains were common on the Santa Fe Trail between Missouri and Santa Fe. The province of Alta California also saw changes. Ship traffic greatly increased, with Boston traders bringing all kinds of goods in exchange for hides and **tallow**. Also, overland traffic to California grew on the Spanish Trail from Santa Fe and the Oregon Trail from Missouri.

Poineers often walked much of the Santa Fe Trail alongside the wagon, which was packed with all their belongings.

On February 28, 1845, the U.S. Congress voted to invite Texas into the union. Mexico protested and broke off relations. In November, President James K. Polk attempted to buy New Mexico and California, but Mexico refused to negotiate. Texas became the 28th state of the United States on December 29, 1845.

In the spring of 1846 President Polk sent General Zachary Taylor with 4,000 troops to camp on the north bank of the Rio Grande, which was **disputed** territory. This provoked Mexican attacks, allowing Polk to declare war on Mexico. It is known

General Zachary Taylor (1784-1850)

as the Mexican War. In June, Polk sent a separate force, the Army of the West, led by General Stephen Watts Kearny, to conquer New Mexico. Kearny and 1,500 troops entered Santa Fe and took it without a fight on August 16. By this time, California had also been taken.

Meanwhile, Taylor moved deeper into Mexico, pushing back Santa Anna. In March 1847, another general, Winfield Scott, landed 10,000 troops on Mexico's eastern coast. He took Veracruz and marched toward the capital, engaging in fierce battles along the way. On September 9, 1847, Scott occupied Mexico City.

Mexico signed the Treaty of Guadalupe Hidalgo on February 2, 1848. It ceded California, New Mexico, and what are now Arizona, Nevada, Utah, Wyoming, Colorado, and parts of Kansas and Oklahoma to the United States. Although Mexico received $15 million for these lands, it gave them up only to avoid losing everything.

When the Duke of Wellington heard of General Scott's success taking Mexico City he called him "the greatest living general."

THE GADSDEN PURCHASE

The Gadsden Purchase was signed in Mexico City .

In 1853, American foreign minister James Gadsden convinced Mexico to sell 30,000 square miles (77,700 square kilometers) of land in what is now southern Arizona and New Mexico. The United States wanted to build a railroad along this route. The Gadsden Purchase filled out the present shape of the **continental** United States along its southern edge.

As the United States grew in prosperity, large numbers of Hispanic people from Mexico migrated across the border to work in agriculture, railroad building, and other industries. Spain ceded one of its last colonies, Puerto Rico, to the United States after losing the Spanish-American War of 1898. By 1910, Puerto Ricans had begun migrating to the United States, mostly to New York, by the thousands.

The blending of all of the cultures that make up the United States, along with the unique contributions of each of those cultures, continues. The offerings that Spain has brought to America, beginning with Christopher Columbus in 1492, are among the richest threads in the intricate tapestry of U.S. history.

Biographies

Many people played important roles throughout this time period. Learn more about them in the Biographies section.

Columbus, Christopher (1451-1506) - Italian explorer in the service of Spain who discovered America for the Europeans in 1492.

Ponce de León, Juan (1460-1521) - Spanish explorer who traveled with Columbus on his second voyage and explored the Florida coast (1513).

Narváez, Pánfilo de (1470-1528) - Spanish conquistador who was commissioned by Carlos V to conquer Florida and was lost at sea.

Pizarro, Francisco (1471-1541) - Leader of the Spanish conquest of Peru (1530-1535).

Cortés, Hernán (1485-1547) - Central figure in the Spanish conquest and colonization of Mexico.

Mendoza, Antonio de (1490-1552) - First viceroy of Nueva España (1535-1550).

Cabeza de Vaca, Alvar Nuñez 1490-1557) - Spanish explorer who was shipwrecked off the Texas coast and was one of the first Europeans to explore the American Southwest.

De Soto, Hernando Méndez (1500-1542) - Spanish adventurer who explored what is now the southeastern United States (1539-1542).

Coronado, Francisco Vásquez de (1510-1554) - Spanish explorer who traveled through the American Southwest (1540-1542).

Menéndez de Avilés, Pedro (1519-1574) - Spanish explorer who established the settlement of St. Augustine, Florida (1565). He became Florida's first Spanish governor.

Drake, Francis (1540-1596) - English sailor and adventurer who raided Spanish ships and colonies in the Caribbean.

Oñate y Salazar, Juan (1549-1624) - Spanish explorer who established the first settlement in Nuevo México (1598).

Popé (1630-1688) - San Juan native who led the successful Pueblo Revolt against the Spanish in 1680.

Carlos III (1716-1788) - King of Spain (1759-1788).

Jefferson, Thomas (1743-1826) - Third president of the United States (1801-1809).

Taylor, Zachary (1784-1850) - Twelfth president of the United States (1849-1850); general who led U.S. troops in the Mexican War (1846-1848).

Santa Anna, Antonio López de (1794-1876) - Mexican general who was defeated by General Winfield Scott in the Mexican War (1846-1848); president of Mexico on several occasions.

Polk, James K. (1795-1849) - The eleventh president of the United States (1845-1849).

Timeline

1492
Christopher Columbus lands on an island in what is now the Bahamas.

1513
Juan Ponce de León sails along present-day United States coast, names the land Pascua Florida or La Florida, and claims it for Spain.

1519-1521
Hernán Cortés defeats the Aztec empire in what is now Mexico.

1531
Francisco Pizarro conquers the Inca empire in present-day Peru.

1539-1543
De Soto expedition through what is now the southeastern United States.

1540-1542
Coronado expedition explores the present-day Southwest.

1610
Founding of Santa Fe, the oldest capital in the United States.

1762-1800
Spain controls the Louisiana Territory.

1763
End of the French and Indian War in which Spain cedes La Florida to England.

1776-1783
The American Revolution gains independence for the English colonies, creating the United States of America. Florida is returned to Spain in 1783.

1803
President Thomas Jefferson purchases Louisiana Territory from France.

1810
The United States takes West Florida over Spain's protests. Mexico begins its struggle for independence.

1819
The United States buys all of Florida from Spain.

1821
Mexico wins independence from Spain; former Spanish colonies are now under Mexico.

1837-1845
Texas declares independence from Mexico and exists as the Lone Star Republic, becoming a U.S. state in 1845.

Spanish Empire in America

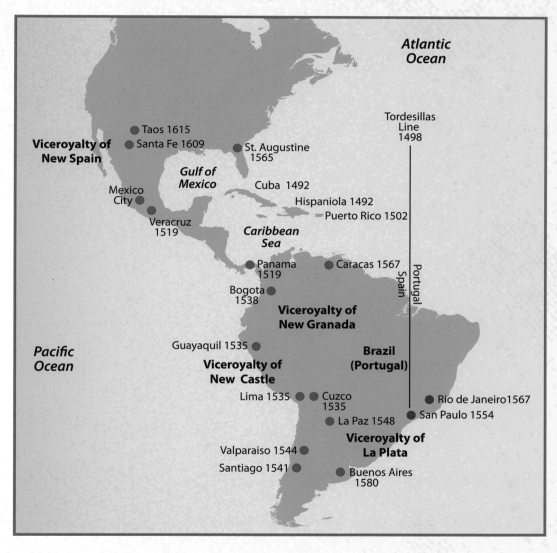

Atlantic Ocean

Viceroyalty of New Spain

Taos 1615
Santa Fe 1609
St. Augustine 1565

Gulf of Mexico

Mexico City

Cuba 1492

Veracruz 1519

Hispaniola 1492
Puerto Rico 1502

Tordesillas Line 1498

Caribbean Sea

Panama 1519
Caracas 1567

Bogota 1538

Portugal
Spain

Viceroyalty of New Granada

Pacific Ocean

Guayaquil 1535

Brazil (Portugal)

Viceroyalty of New Castle

Lima 1535
Cuzco 1535

Rio de Janeiro 1567
San Paulo 1554

La Paz 1548

Viceroyalty of La Plata

Valparaiso 1544

Santiago 1541

Buenos Aires 1580

Websites to Visit

www.kidinfo.com/american_history/spanish_american_war.html

www.socialstudiesforkids.com/articles/.../juanponcedeleon1.htm

www.kidport.com/reflib/usahistory/frenchindian/frenindwar.htm

Show What You Know

1. When did Christopher Columbus land on what is now known as the Bahamas?

2. What is another name for the French and Indian War?

3. What was the original name for the Alamo?

4. What is the oldest capital city in the United States?

5. In what year did Ponce de León first see the Florida shores?

Glossary

annexation (AN-eks-a-shuhn): attachment of something, such as a territory, to something larger, such as a state or country

barter (BAHR-tur): to trade by exchanging wares rather than money

buffer (BUHF-ur): a device used as a cushion against damage or shock

colonist (KAH-uh-nist): a person who establishes a colony

conquistador (KAHN-kweest-uh-dawr): spanish for conqueror; a leader in the Spanish conquest of America

continental (KAHN-tuh-nuhnt-uhl): relating to a continent, one of the great divisions of land on the globe

convert (KAHN-vurt): to convince a person to change beliefs; a person who has been brought over from one belief to another

criollo (KRYE-oh-luh): a person of pure Spanish descent born in America

drought (drout): a prolonged period of dryness

fortress (FOR-tris): stronghold; large fortification

friar (frye-uhr): a member of a religious order dedicated to poverty and engaging in religious activity

immunity (i-MYOON-uh-tee): the ability to resist a particular disease

maraud (muh-rahwd): to roam about and raid in search of goods to steal

mestizo (meh-STEE-zoh): a person of mixed European and Native American ancestry

ministry (MIN-i-stree): the functions of a minister, or one who directs church worship; a group of such ministers

Pope (pohp): the head of the Roman Catholic Church, whose headquarters is Vatican City in Rome

presidio (pre-si-dee-oh): a military post or fortified settlement

sect (sekt): a subgroup of a religion

skirmish (SKUR-mish): a minor fight or a minor battle in a larger war

tallow (TAL-ow): the white, solid fat of cattle or sheep, which is processed and used in candles and soap

viceroy (VYE-suh-roy): the governor of a country or province who rules as a king's representative

Index